Everyday Life

Moira Butterfield

This edition published in 2013 by Franklin Watts

Copyright © Franklin Watts 2013

Franklin Watts
338 Euston Road
London NW1 3BH

Franklin Watts Australia
Level 17/207 Kent Street
Sydney NSW 2000

A CIP catalogue record for this book
is available from the British Library.

Dewey number: 942.05

ISBN 978 1 4451 1857 4

Printed in China

Franklin Watts is a division of Hachette Children's Books,
an Hachette UK company

www.hachette.co.uk

Designer: Jason Billin
Editor: Sarah Ridley
Art director: Jonathan Hair
Editor-in-chief: John C. Miles
Picture research: Diana Morris

Note to parents and teachers:
Every effort has been made by the Publishers to ensure
that the websites in this book are suitable for children, that
they are of the highest educational value, and that they
contain no inappropriate or offensive material. However,
because of the nature of the Internet, it is impossible to
guarantee that the contents of these sites will not be
altered. We strongly advise that Internet access is
supervised by a responsible adult.

Picture credits
Adams Picture Library/Alamy: 6
Bibliothèque Nationale, Paris/Bridgeman Art Library: 13
T Alena Brett: 4, 25
British Library, London/Bridgeman Art Library: 11
British Museum, London/HIP/Topfoto: 12
Burghley House,Stamford/ Mark Fiennes/Bridgeman Art
Library: 9
Mary Evans Picture Library: 17
Geoffrey Frosh/NTPL: 19
Hatfield House, Hertfordshire/Bridgeman Art Library:
cover, 1, 15
David Levenson/NTPL: 20
Longleat House, Wiltshire/Bridgeman Art Library: 14
Musée des Beaux-Arts, Lille/Bridgeman Art Library: 18
The Museum of London: 24
Museum of London/Bridgeman Art Library: 21
Private Collection/Bridgeman Art Library: 8, 10, 22, 23,
26, 29
Private Collection/© Philip Mould, Historical Portraits Ltd,
London/Bridgeman Art Library: 5
Ben Ramos/Alamy: 16
Society of Antiquaries/Bridgeman Art Library: 3, 7
V&A Images: 28
Woodmansterne/Topfoto: 27

*Every attempt has been made to clear copyright. Should there
be any inadvertent omission please apply to the publisher for
rectification.*

Contents

Tudor kings and queens

The Tudor age began in 1485 when the King of England, Richard III, was defeated at the Battle of Bosworth by a rival nobleman called Henry Tudor. Henry was crowned King Henry VII.

Henry, father and son

Henry VII's reign was peaceful and he was known for spending money carefully. His son, Henry VIII, had a much more event-filled reign and brought religious unrest to the country by passing laws to split the Church of England from the Roman Catholic Church (see pages 24–25). He is famous for marrying six times. He divorced two of his wives and executed two more. One wife died after childbirth and one survived him.

King Henry VIII

Edward VI

Henry's son Edward VI was nine years old when he became king. He was clever and people had high hopes for him, but he was also sickly, and he died at the age of 16. He was succeeded by his eldest sister Mary.

Mary I and Elizabeth I

Mary I was a devout Roman Catholic and tried to undo the religious changes her father and brother had made. She died childless in 1558 and her sister Elizabeth became queen. Elizabeth I reigned for 44 years, but she never married or had children, so she was the last of the Tudor monarchs to rule England. Her cousin James Stuart, King of Scotland, succeeded her in 1603 and began the rule of the Stuart kings and queens.

Queen Elizabeth I

Tudors from top to bottom

In Tudor times society was organised in strict ranks. Everybody had to obey the monarch, who was all-powerful. Nobles were the next most important people, followed by merchants and businessmen, then craftsmen and farmers. Under them were servants and labourers, and at the bottom there were the homeless and unemployed.

Growing towns

During Tudor times more and more people began to move from the countryside to towns and cities.

Smelly city life

Lots of new town houses were built in Tudor times, sometimes crowded together in narrow streets. People often worked and lived in the same place, with a workshop or a shop on the ground floor and rooms above. They poured their waste out of the window into the dirty stinking streets and there was no drainage, so towns and cities were dirty smelly places and diseases spread quickly.

Escape to the country

London was the largest Tudor city. It was a busy port and government centre and lots of people moved there to find work. But in the summer months the heat made the city stink. It was unhealthy, so wealthy people preferred to escape to a second home in the countryside.

These Tudor houses are in the town of Lavenham in Suffolk.

Busy and fun

Many towns and cities doubled in size in Tudor times. They were lively places, with shops, workshops, taverns, churches and regular markets for buying and selling goods and farm animals. Travelling actors would tour the towns and cities, putting on shows (see page 29). In London there was the chance to see regular Royal events such as processions, weddings and sometimes executions, too.

An Italian's view

"All the streets are so badly paved that they get wet at the slightest quantity of water. Then a vast amount of evil-smelling mud is formed, which does not disappear quickly but lasts a long time, in fact nearly the whole year round. The citizens, therefore, in order to remove this mud and filth from their boots, are accustomed to spread fresh rushes on the floors of all houses..." Andreas Franciscus, an Italian visiting London in 1497.

This view of London shows part of Edward VI's coronation procession from the Tower of London (far left) to Westminster in 1547. Old St Paul's Cathedral is the building with the spire (far right).

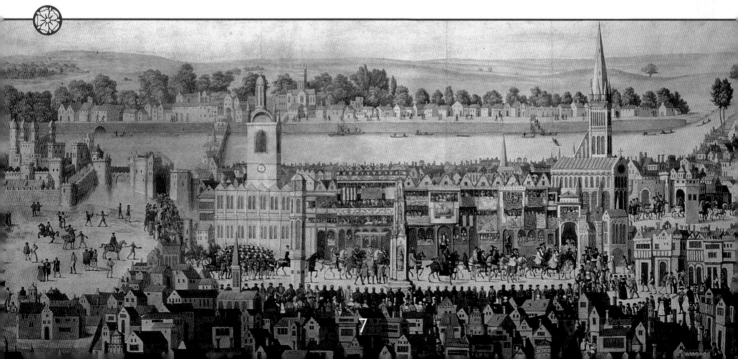

Country life

Though towns were growing, most people still lived in the countryside. Ordinary people often lived their whole lives in the same village.

Noble owners

The land in the countryside was usually owned by nobles. Sometimes farmers managed to buy their own land but usually they had to rent it. Farm workers were paid a small wage or given food and housing in exchange for work.

Smoky and small

Most villagers lived in small wooden houses owned by their landlord. The whole family usually crammed into one or two dark rooms, with a wood fire to keep them warm. As many houses didn't have a proper chimney, the rooms would have been filled with smoke from the fire. There was hardly any furniture and people slept on straw-filled mattresses.

Tudor village houses were often made of wood. Only chimneys were made of brick or stone.

Luxury life

Life was more comfortable for rich landowners. Many built grand houses on their country estates, with luxury features such as big kitchens and lots of fireplaces with chimneys. They imported (brought in) ideas from abroad, such as glass windows, elegant statues and beautiful gardens.

Burghley House in Lincolnshire is one of the grandest country houses of the Tudor era. It was built during the reign of Mary I.

Getting around

The countryside in Tudor times wasn't as cut off as you might think. There was a network of roads, known as the King's Highway, that linked the major towns. Horses were very expensive and poor people had to walk everywhere, and so rarely travelled very far.

On the farm

Farming was the main way of making a living in the countryside. Most people worked as farm labourers for the local landowners.

Working the land

Being a farm labourer was hard work. Everything had to be done by hand or with the help of horses or oxen. Seeds had to be planted by hand and at harvest time the fields were filled with people cutting the crop using curved knives called sickles.

The sheep arrive

The wool industry was growing, and in some parts of the country landowners started to turn their fields into grazing land for sheep, because they could make lots of money from the wool. They needed fewer farm workers to do this type of work. They also built walls around their property to keep the sheep in, which meant there was

A Tudor illustration showing farm labourers ploughing with oxen.

less land for villagers to use for grazing their own animals. Many country people found life much harder because of the changes.

Weavers and craftsmen

Some country workers were skilled craftsmen. They made leather goods such as shoes and horse saddles, or iron objects such as farm tools and horse shoes. As the wool industry grew, more people learnt how to spin and weave wool into cloth.

Shepherding was a traditional job in the countryside. These shepherds are shearing (cutting the wool off) their sheep.

Bad harvests

Today much of our food can be imported (brought in) from abroad, but back in Tudor times a poor harvest due to bad weather meant that people sometimes died from hunger. We know from diaries of the time that there were often serious food shortages.

Making and selling

Many people began to grow wealthy by making goods and selling them, sometimes to other countries.

Guilds of workers

Craftsmen who made goods joined groups called guilds. The guilds had rules about how people should be trained and set a standard for their work. Guilds also helped their members if they were ill and weren't able to work. Young boys who wanted to be craftsmen became apprentices, which meant they lived and worked with an employer to learn their trade.

Apprentices at work in a Tudor goldsmith's workshop.

Go and visit

At the Guildhall in Lavenham, Suffolk, you can find out how cloth was made and see a Tudor garden filled with plants that were made into dye to colour the wool.

Tudor industries

Glass-making, soap-making and sugar-refining (making raw sugar into edible sugar) were all important Tudor industries. They all needed fires for their work, so mines opened up in some parts of the country to provide coal for burning. Unlike modern industries, there was no machinery to help with industrial work and much of it was dangerous.

Reading and writing jobs

Girls were not normally taught, but bright boys went to grammar schools (see page 16). They might become clerks, bankers, priests, teachers or work in the new trade of printing and bookselling.

This picture shows paper sheets being made by hand to use in books.

Beggars are bad

Jobless people were called "vagrants" or "vagabonds". They were seen as dangerous and threatening. Laws were brought in to control them and to ban begging.

Family life

The family was seen as very important in Tudor times.

Getting married

People from wealthy families usually married early, maybe as early as 12 for a girl, or 14 for a boy. Often their parents decided who they would marry, usually someone from a rich family like their own. Ordinary people often waited longer to get married, to earn enough money to set up their own home.

A portrait of Lord Cobham and his family. Wealthy families had many children, often up to 12.

Working wives

Women were considered less important than men, and they were expected to run the household and look after children under the rule of their husband. Many poor women also worked on the land or at home doing jobs such as spinning and weaving. Wealthy women had servants to run their homes.

A skimmington ride

As a punishment for wrongdoing in a marriage, such as wife-beating or nagging, local villagers sometimes dragged out a husband, wife or both and forced them to go on a noisy procession called a "skimmington ride", to shame them.

Men in power

Men were seen as the head of the family, and usually owned all the property, which they passed down to other males in their family when they died. The Tudors believed that God ruled the universe, the monarch ruled the country and a husband ruled his family.

This painting shows a wealthy Tudor wedding at Bermondsey, near London.

Tudor children

Tudor parents were much stricter than parents today, and they regularly beat their children.

No school for you

Very poor children did not go to school, but were expected to work as soon as they were old enough. Most girls did not go to school, either. They learnt homemaking skills instead, such as cooking and sewing. A few wealthy girls learnt reading and writing from tutors (private teachers).

Boys get more

Boys from very wealthy families had their own private tutors, paid for by their parents. Boys from less well-off families sometimes got the

Go and visit

The Tudor Edward VI Grammar School in Stratford-upon-Avon has been a school since Tudor times. The playwright William Shakespeare was once a pupil there. It is still a working school, but it is sometimes open to visitors.

chance to go to a daily grammar school from the age of seven, which was free if they won a scholarship (passed an exam). Henry VIII opened the first grammar schools in England, called King's Schools. School life was strict, and the teachers carried bundles of birch twigs tied together like a broom, to beat any pupils who disobeyed the rules.

Toys and games

Poor children played with homemade wooden toys such as spinning tops, while wealthier ones might have a rocking horse or a doll. Inflated pig's bladders made good footballs, and pebbles were used to play marbles. Team games such as blindman's buff and leapfrog were popular, too.

A painting of a Tudor schoolroom. The children had to speak in Latin. Their teacher watches over them strictly.

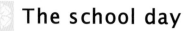 **The school day**

Schoolboys spent most of their time learning Latin. The school day was long: from 6 am until 5.30 pm, six days a week.

Mealtimes

Rich people could afford three meals a day, but poorer people had to manage with less.

Time to eat

Everybody ate lots of bread, and well-off families ate plenty of meat, fish and dairy products, too. Poor families ate a kind of vegetable soup called pottage, sometimes adding hunks of meat for a treat. Wealthy people looked down on vegetables as being an inferior food for the poor, not realising they were actually healthy to eat.

This painting gives a good idea of what a Tudor kitchen looked like. Meat was roasted on spits in front of the fire.

Big banquets

Rich people had a reputation for eating too much. At the court of Henry VIII it wasn't unusual to have banquets with ten different courses, including luxury foods such as venison or even roast swan. In 1541 a new law tried to stop people eating too much. The law stated that nobles were allowed a maximum of seven dishes at a meal, gentlemen could eat five dishes and everyone else could have just four dishes.

A large fire would have warmed diners as they ate in the hall of Sutton House in London. Exotic carpets from the Middle East were an expensive luxury used to cover the tables.

Sweet foods

The Tudors liked their food sweet, and honey was used in many meat dishes, as well as in biscuits and pies. Only wealthy people could afford sugar, and they thought it was a great luxury. They didn't know that it rotted their teeth.

 Go and visit

At Hampton Court Palace in London you can see the huge kitchens used to create banquets for Henry VIII.

Clothes and fashion

In Tudor times clothes were a sign of how important and wealthy someone was.

Fashion by law

Clothing was so important that in 1510 Parliament passed a law stating what everybody should wear. If anybody disobeyed they could be fined or punished. Only the royal family could wear gold cloth or anything purple. Servants, labourers and farmers were not allowed to use material that cost over a given amount. Nor were they allowed to wear gold rings.

Tudor clothes for ordinary people were often made from a coarse brown woollen fabric.

Ordinary clothing

Ordinary people often only owned one set of clothes, homemade from linen or wool and often blue or brown. They also wore linen underclothes, which stopped their outer clothes getting too sweaty. Working women wore long dresses of plain cloth over woollen

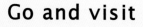 Go and visit

The Victoria and Albert Museum in London has a huge collection of historical clothes. Also, look out for Tudor re-enactments in your local area. At Kentwell Hall, in Suffolk, people of all ages gather to act out Tudor life.

stockings, and working men wore a loose wool tunic over breeches (long shorts) and stockings. Somebody more important, such as a merchant or a clerk, would wear a long gown. Children were usually dressed as mini-adults.

Go and visit

Hall i' th' Wood is a museum based in Bolton, Greater Manchester. It hosts events where you can dress up in 16th century-style clothes.

Clothes for the wealthy were made from rich fabrics, like these examples in the Victoria and Albert Museum.

Pale is beautiful

It was fashionable for the wealthy to be pale skinned because it showed you were rich enough not to have to work outdoors. Women used potions and make-up to help them keep their skins as white as possible, including a face powder made from white lead. They did not realise that the lead was poisonous and badly damaged their skin.

21

Health and medicine

Most Tudors died before they reached the age of 50. As many as one in five children died within their first year of life.

Dirty diseases

The reason so many people died young was because nobody understood how diseases were spread. One of the biggest problems was cleanliness. People hardly ever washed, and this made it easy for the disease of typhus to spread because it passed from one person to the next on body lice. Dysentery, called "the flux", was a common illness passed through drinking dirty water.

Tudor doctors

If you were ill you could pay for a physician, a surgeon or an apothecary to help, but poor people usually saw a wise woman (see panel).

This picture shows someone having a leg amputated (sawn off). There were no painkillers and no antibiotics to stop infection afterwards.

The "royal touch"

Scrofula — a disease of the neck — was treated not by doctors or wise women, but by the monarch. People believed that kings and queens had special holy powers to cure this illness simply by touching the patient. Sufferers came to special church services to get the "royal touch". In the picture on the right, Mary I is shown at a church service touching somebody with scrofula.

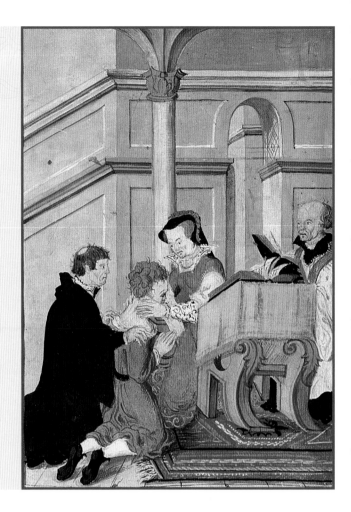

Physicians were the best-educated medical people but they often tried blood-letting — cutting a patient to let a lot of blood flow into a cup. This often made the poor patient weaker. Surgeons could set broken bones and amputate (cut off) limbs, but they did it without painkillers, so their patient suffered badly. Apothecaries sold herbal cures, though often these were useless or made people even more ill.

Wise women

Wise women treated illnesses using cures made of natural ingredients; recipes passed down by word of mouth from their mothers or grandmothers. Some of these cures sound very strange today. They included using the body of a mouse to treat warts or toothache, and using a paste made of mashed mole to cure baldness!

Trouble in church

Most Tudor people believed in God, but not everybody worshipped the same way.

Follow the monarch

People were expected to agree with their monarch on religion. To disagree was a serious crime called "heresy". When Henry VIII became king he was a Roman Catholic, which meant he went to church services held in Latin and followed the teachings of the Pope, the head of the Roman Catholic Church

A set of 16th-century sacred objects (with their case) for Roman Catholic worship — a bottle for holy wine, a chalice (cup) and a paten (communion plate).

based in Rome. People were expected to follow the king's example, even though most of them couldn't understand Latin.

Breaking with Rome

In 1532 Henry VIII wanted to divorce his first wife, Catherine of Aragon, and marry Anne Boleyn. He hoped she would give birth to a male heir to succeed him. The Pope refused to agree to the divorce, so Henry declared himself the Head of the Church of England and granted his own divorce. Loyal Catholics disagreed with the king's actions and religious rows began.

Church trouble

Across Europe people began to argue about the right way to worship God and a new faith called Protestantism was set up. Henry's daughter Mary I was a Catholic who hated Protestants and had some of them burned. Her sister, Elizabeth I, was a Protestant, and there were several Catholic plots to try and overthrow her during her reign.

An English Bible

William Tyndale was a preacher who translated the Bible into English. He wanted everyone to be able to read it for themselves, but at first Henry VIII banned his work and Tyndale had to leave the country. Later Henry changed his mind and ordered that there should be a copy of Tyndale's English Bible in every church in England. For many, this was the first time they had ever read the Bible for themselves.

Mary I (reigned 1553–1558) ordered the execution of hundreds of Protestants.

Crime and punishment

There were violent punishments for crimes in Tudor times.

Down in the dungeons

Criminals were thrown into stinking dark dungeons with heavy doors and small barred windows. Sometimes the cells were flooded or crawling with hungry rats. Torture was used to get confessions, and the most feared torture was stretching on the rack. The prisoner's legs and arms were tied to ropes fixed to a wooden frame. Then ropes were slowly turned to stretch the victim's limbs until their joints popped out of their sockets.

A true defcription of the racking and cruell handling of *Cutbert Simfon in the Tower.*

The grating of an arrowe through Cutbert Simfons fingers,

Cutbert Simfon vpon the rack.

A picture of Cuthbert Simson being tortured on the rack for being a Protestant during the reign of Mary I. Many Catholics were tortured this way during Elizabeth I's reign.

Burned alive

"1541: In this yere was burned in Smithfield, a child named Richard Mekins, this child passed not the age of XV [15] yeres, and somewhat as he had heard some other folks talke, chaunced to speake against the Sacrament of the aultar."
Edward Hall, writing in his *Chronicles*, 1541, on the burning of a boy for questioning Roman Catholic worship.

The stocks and other punishments

Thieves were sometimes whipped or placed in a wooden trap called the stocks. Anyone could throw rotten food at the criminal as he sat outdoors in the stocks. Wrongdoers could also be sentenced to have a hand or an ear chopped off. A law passed in 1572 ordered that vagrants (homeless beggars) should be punished by being whipped, or branded (burnt) on the ear. The death sentence was common, too. Burnings and hangings were public events that anyone could come to watch.

A set of village stocks with holes for trapping and locking someone's legs in place.

Having fun

On public holidays and church festival days there was time for fun and games.

Sports and parties

Sports such as hunting with dogs and falconry (hunting with birds) were popular pastimes for the rich. Henry VIII loved jousting — a sport where knights tried to knock each other off their horses using lances. He also played a kind of early tennis called "real tennis". Dancing and music were very popular at the Royal court, and Henry VIII even wrote his own music and poetry.

This embroidered scene shows Tudor nobles hunting.

Beer buildings

In Tudor times taverns and ale houses became popular. If you just wanted a drink of beer you would go to an ale house. If you wanted food as well, you would visit a tavern. Both places were well known for being noisy, drunken spots where fights broke out. An inn was more like a hotel, where you could get a room and stabling for a horse as well as food and drink.

Football and fighting

Public holidays were times for working people to dance, eat and drink, and join in sports such as football. There was no limit to the number of people who could play football, and no proper rules either. The ball was made from a pig's bladder and the goalposts could be miles apart. The Tudors also liked cruel sports such as bear-baiting (a chained-up bear forced to fight dogs) or cock-fighting (cockerels fighting each other to the death).

Plays and the theatre

In towns and villages people gathered to see plays performed by travelling actors. The stories they acted were often based on the Bible or ancient myths. Theatres opened for the first time in London, and we know that Elizabeth I enjoyed watching plays. Women were not allowed to act, though. The female parts were played by boy actors.

29

Glossary

apprentice
A person who learns a trade by being employed in it for an agreed period of time at a low wage.

clerk
A person employed in an office, bank or shop, to keep records and accounts.

cock-fighting
A cruel blood sport where two cockerels fight each other to the death. Onlookers placed bets on which cockerel would win.

dysentery
A disease of the intestines that causes severe, bloody diarrhoea.

grammar schools
Schools that were originally founded in the 16th century to teach Latin grammar.

heir
Someone who will be given money, property or a title when somebody else dies.

heresy
A belief or practice that is different to what is normally accepted.

holy day
A religious festival.

jousting
A contest between two knights, riding horses and carrying lances. Each knight tries to knock the other off his horse.

lease
To enter an agreement with a landowner to use his land for a certain amount of time.

Mass
A Roman Catholic church service.

merchant
Somebody who sells goods for profit. Often they trade with other countries.

ornate
Highly decorated.

plague
A deadly disease that spreads quickly over a large area.

Protestants
Christians who rejected the authority of the Roman Catholic Church and the Pope in Rome and instead focused on scripture as the best way to worship God.

revised
Changed and updated.

Roman Catholic
Christians who believe that the Pope in Rome is the head of their religion.

sickle
A handle with a sharp curved blade used to cut stalks of corn.

stocks
A device to punish people by trapping their legs so that they cannot move.

stonemasons
People who are skilled in cutting and using stone.

treason
The crime of betraying your country or plotting against the king or queen.

Timeline

22 August 1485 Henry Tudor becomes King Henry VII.

21 April 1509 His son, also Henry Tudor, becomes King Henry VIII of England.

17 November 1534 The Act of Supremacy is passed by Parliament. It declares the English monarch to be the Supreme Head of the Church of England.

19 May 1536 King Henry VIII's second wife, Anne Boleyn, is executed.

12 October 1537 King Henry VIII's only son, Prince Edward, is born.

28 January 1547 Edward Tudor becomes King Edward VI.

3 August 1553 Mary Tudor becomes Queen Mary I.

25 July 1554 Queen Mary I marries King Philip II of Spain.

17 November 1558 Elizabeth Tudor becomes Queen Elizabeth I.

19 June 1566 King James VI of Scotland is born.

24 March 1603 Queen Elizabeth I dies; King James VI of Scotland becomes King of England.

Websites

http://www.tudorbritain.org/
A site for children learning about the Tudors, created by the Victoria and Albert Museum.

http://www.geffrye-museum.org.uk/kidszone/garden/
Have fun designing your own Elizabethan garden.

http://www.museumoflondon.org.uk/learning/features_facts/targettudors/index.html
Learn more about everyday life in Tudor times.

http://www.maryrose.org/explore/menu.htm
Get some hands-on experience of the Tudor age when you join the crew of the Tudor warship the *Mary Rose*.

http://www.woodlands-junior.kent.sch.uk/Homework/tudors/dailylife.htm
A site designed especially for primary school children studying the Tudors.

Index